MUSIC MINUS ONE DRUMMER

Night • Summertime • Chickory Stick
Short Ballad • Blue Bossa
Serenity • Revelation
Poolside Blues • Count Me In

5013

OPEN SESSION

with the
Greg Burrows Quintet

EVANS
RESONANT

2

MMO CD 5013
2 CD Set

mmo
Music Minus One

OPEN SESSION WITH THE GREG BURROWS QUINTET

Stylistic focus

The focus of this new Music Minus One for Drummers package is in the following styles of jazz playing:

- Straight ahead feel, medium (Serenity)
- Straight ahead, uptempo (Chickory Stick, Night)
- Ballad w/brushes /sticks (Short Ballad)
- Latin (Afro-Cuban, Salsa) (Summertime)
- Brazil (Bossa Nova/Samba: Blue Bossa, Revelation)
- Drum Solo feature (Count Me In)
- Classic "Blakey"-style shuffle (Poolside Blues)

This is the standard range of styles which are expected to be familiar to the drummer in almost any acoustic jazz setting. These are the basic tools and they are presented here with clear, straightforward charts and helpful instructional notes in the accompanying book for those who have no background in certain areas.

Jazz drumming is no longer an art which primarily requires the drummer to go "ding ding-da ding" on the ride cymbal with punctuation on the snare and bass drums with the occasional "Latin" tune for variety. It is an ever-expanding art. The only unbending rule of the game is that every ounce of it must SWING. How to define "swing" to the drum student?

Basically, swing is a difficult thing to describe verbally. It is an essence and a feeling and any good musician knows when it is happening or not. In earlier times it was connected to dancing: if the music doesn't make you want to move your feet, it ain't swinging. But during the Bebop era [late 1940's through the early 1950's] and beyond, swing took on a deeper meaning and began to relate on many levels. Are the musicians on the same level conceptually? Do you feel like shouting and clapping for a solo or would you rather be home watching The Weather Channel? These are a few of the questions to which, if the answer is "no," then it is not swinging.

There are no shortcuts to achieving this innate sense of swing in your playing. It takes years of practice, experience playing with a variety of ensembles, many hours of informal jam sessions, and a lot of hours of deep listening to the classic jazz recordings (the Miles Davis Quintets of the 50's and 60's come to mind). Once you've begun the process, it becomes an ever-deepening and enjoyable experience which can be full of surprises. I myself have been playing for nearly thirty years, and feel as though I am at the "tip of the iceberg" when it comes to learning about and understanding this wonderful music.

And speaking of icebergs, keep in mind that along the way many great musicians have become human "Titanics". Take care of your health and avoid bad habits so that you can enjoy a long and fulfilling journey as a drummer! Music has a therapeutic ability to make you feel great.

It is my sincere belief that incorporating CD programs such as this one into your daily practice routine can be a very helpful way to improve your inner swing feel as well as your ability as a musical team player. Enjoy, and see you in the next one.

Greg Burrows

4

Introduction & Personal Profile

Welcome to Music Minus One's "Open Session with the Greg Burrows Quintet". The following is a brief introduction to the package as well as some personal background on myself. Thank you for making this purchase. I am proud to be a part of the MMO legacy since I used to practice along with and learn chart-reading using records made by this same company. It feels nice to "give something back" to a company which provided me with so many educational stepping stones, and I hope you find this package useful.

What you hold in your hands is a play-along CD, a full band CD with original drum tracks, and accompanying charts with helpful written information. The recordings were designed for use by intermediate to advanced level students of jazz drumming, and of drumming in general. I hope that it is also of some use for professionals who wish to brush up on their jazz chops, or who simply wish to have a vehicle for playing in the privacy of their practice rooms. The players who joined me in performing this fine collection of great tunes are among the best players on New York's Jazz scene. I chose the players based on their overall musicality, experience, and in their ability to contribute as composers/arrangers. Everyone delivered, and played from their hearts and souls. Bear in mind while playing with the songs: should you feel a need to hear more of the bass player in your headphones (and I do suggest using headphones when playing with the CD's whenever possible to really get yourself inside of the rhythm section) turn up the bass level on the stereo system. If the horns are interfering with your cymbal work, cut the treble level. In this way, you can "EQ" the music yourself to some degree. Also, let me clarify that CD #1 is for listening and analyzing the full band presentation, while CD#2 is your opportunity to "sit in" and run the music with the band yourself, since the drum tracks are almost totally removed from the sonic picture.

Note: You will notice when listening carefully that you will hear a "ghost image" of the original drum tracks, but once you start playing along this will not pose any distraction to your efforts. Your drumming will "mask" what little remains of the pre-existing drums. We recorded these tunes completely "live" and so as a result, it was impossible to achieve 100% isolation of the drums without putting me in another room altogether! This, of course, would not be practical since Jazz is music of communication, eye contact amongst players, and group connection.

GREG BURROWS' PERSONAL BACKGROUND

I am originally from New Haven, Connecticut and grew up in New Rochelle, about a 5 minute drive from the outer limits of New York City. New Rochelle is a fertile and diverse place to grow up for a musician because there is tremendous racial diversity there. One of my favorite childhood memories is the period in which I played drums with a local Gospel choir at thirteen years of age. We would do these "mini tours" of Black churches throughout the area, and it was highly unusual for White musicians to be mingling and performing in this setting, but sure enough, the alto sax player and I were of Caucasian descent, and there we were making strong and entrancing Spiritual music, all of us together.

I took up the drums in earnest at about age 9, when on that birthday my parents purchased a set of old calf-skinned parade drums (I believe they were ancient Ludwigs, and the tenor drum even had the original gut snares!). By that time I'd already demolished a little kiddy set, which was given to me as a gift at age seven. Thank God for tolerant neighbors and an understanding family!!!

Eventually, in my teens I began more serious studies and also started playing a local Rock & Roll band at parties and high school dances. There were also often bebop jam sessions going on as New Rochelle had a small but fertile Jazz scene. The group that I played with during my early teen years, Diogenes, was gaining a reputation as a smokin' little group (just ask Joe DiGiorgi, the engineer of these MMO sessions - he was the group's lead guitarist), and we would often play a two-chord jam such as The Doors' "Light My Fire" for as long as 45 minutes. This was the creative environment which had enabled me to explore and blossom in unusual ways, since by that time (the mid-seventies) rock music "regulations" had reverted back to a 3½-minute limit on song length.

It was also at around this time that I'd discovered the amazing drumming of Elvin Jones, "Philly" Joe Jones, Mel Lewis, Al Foster, Steve Gadd, and other master musicians in the Jazz vein. After hearing these miraculous sounds for the first time, especially Elvin, I was transformed; I felt as though I'd found a musical "gold mine".

My private studies included lessons with Henry Adler, Glen Berino, Dave Weckl, Gary Chester, and Peter Erskine. I had also spent two years as a Percussion Major at S.U.N.Y. College at Puchase studying mallet percussion, 20th Century multiple percussion, and tympani with Ray DesRoches and others. This period was a crucial formative time for me as a musician because I was simultaneously learning the deep musical and technical requirements of Classical percussion as well as beginning my professional career as a player.

My humble advice to the drummers of the 90's and into the 21st Century is that one must keep an open mind and open ears. As the world becomes "smaller" it seems appropriate to learn and understand the musics of many cultures, not only that which you find in your own back yard. Take a moment to listen to African music, Arabic, Israeli, Japanese, Brazilian, and so on and on. There is a fantastic world of drumming going on out there, and the more you check it out the more you can pull into your own playing and give yourself a unique edge. For example, the fantastic drummer from the Police, Stewart Copeland, was heavily influenced by the rhythms of Lebanon, because he'd lived there as a child. As a result, he sounds like absolutely no one else on the instrument and has a style he can truly call his own. This is the highest possible aspiration for today's drummers - to search fearlessly for their own personal sound.

I sincerely hope that this package assists you in continuing on your journey, that you enjoy the musical challenges contained herein, and learn something useful from it. On behalf of Music Minus One I thank you for purchasing this educational tool. Please take the time to check out some of the other fantastic releases by this company and keep an eye out for future releases by yours truly. Thank you.

Greg Burrows

Greg can be contacted via e-mail at: bonobo123@aol.com

Concepts and performance tips: This is a fun and challenging piece from the drummer's standpoint (or any player for that matter) because of the unusual placement of accents, and the atypical solo form. It is important to keep relaxed physically while playing this style because there could be a tendency to "overdo it" in keeping up the drive and forward momentum of the tune; make sure to always serve the groove when drumming on a tune like this. That is one of the secrets behind that elusive rhythmic element we call SWING...the balance of keeping it both driving yet settled, exciting yet controlled, all at the same time!

This is also a wonderful opportunity to apply one of the fundamental "rules" of playing this music: always bring the dynamic level DOWN at the beginning of a solo (with rare exceptions.) For example, after the opening melody (the "head",) come way down in volume to enable the soloist whom you are supporting to "go somewhere", to make a state-ment (in this particular case it is Todd Anderson's tenor sax solo, followed by piano.) If you come out bashing from the beginning of each solo, you are left only with the option to a): continually bash thoughtlessly throughout the solo, or b): to gradually drop in level and energy. Neither one of these approaches would really create exciting and interesting music.

Background on the song and the arrangement: Our pianist Kevin Hays cooked up this composition expressly for this session; I'd requested of him an uptempo swing kind of thing and he went beyond the call when composing 'Night'. During rehearsals he was searching for a good spot in the tune for a drum solo and it struck me [no pun intended] that there was no need for that, since in a sense the whole thing is a "drum feature" - it's an opportunity for the drummer to negotiate the accent scheme while keeping the pulse cooking throughout.

Night

Uptempo Swing

drum charts by Greg Burrows & William Bausch
[Track 1]

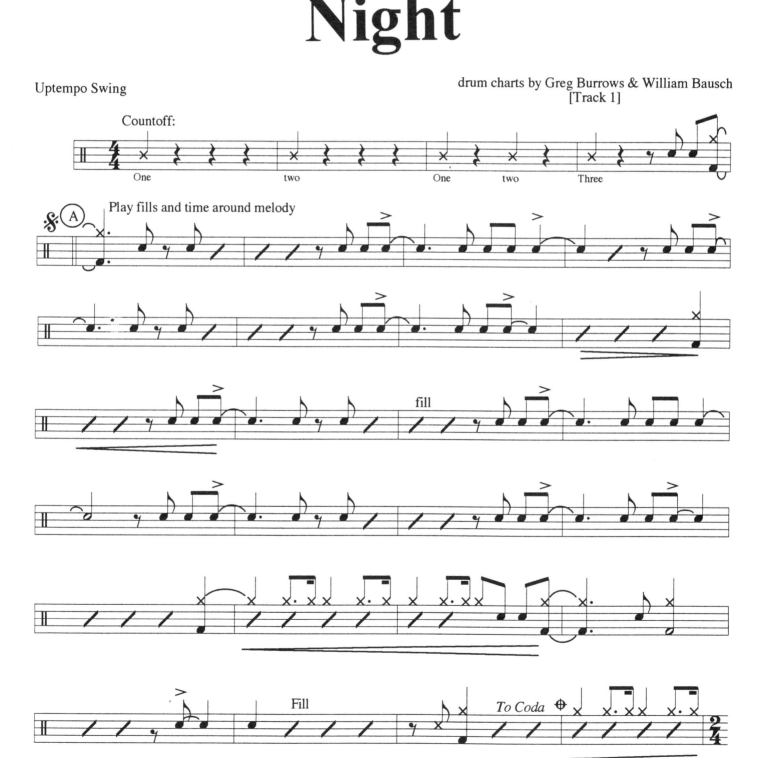

SOLOS: Play time --Hits 1st x only

D.S. al Coda

Coda

Concepts and performance tips: You will need to have a cowbell on your setup for this strongly Latin-flavored tune; if you don't have one available, the bell of your ride cymbal is sufficient. The feeling of this tune is reminiscent of the great Latin bands of the 50's-60's, as featured in the music of Dizzy Gillespie, Cal Tjader, Tito Puente, and others. I don't make any claims that this is a true Latin rendition, though Salaam's conga work (and other percussion, including bongo bell and guiro) helps to enhance the feeling, as well as bongo overdubs by me.

Traditionally, this style does not utilize the drumset; usually the drumming is covered by a large percussion section. However, there are master players who have brought the instrument more strongly into the picture, such as Robbie Ameen and others. Dave Weckl and has also done magnificent work in this area [check out recordings he's done with French Toast or Michel Camilo in the 80's], and Joel Rosenblatt as well [also Michel Camilo, and Spyro Gyra]. Take some time to hear the work of these players if you haven't already; their playing is very inspirational and can help give you ideas in approaching this challenging style of drumming.

The key to making this one happen is to stick strongly to the quarter note pulse on the cowbell; this creates a feel similar to a cha-cha rhythm. I played on the top side of a large mambo bell attached to my bass drum, as opposes to playing at the mouth of the bell - a lighter sound. Also, I suggest that you learn some of the grooves that I am incorporating in the song, either through using the provided drum charts or listening to my work on the full-band CD.

One of the tricky things about this style is that the bass drum is rarely played on "one"(see charts), which may be a good thing to practice separately from the disc. Also, I suggest keeping the snares off in order to achieve a timbale-like effect. In Salsa and other Latin music, the timbale player signals section changes and in a larger sense leads the band. I didn't stick to that concept as a rule, since this is more of a Jazz rendition and a tribute than an attempt at "authentic" Latin drumming.

During the drum solo section (which follows the sax and piano solos and ensemble chorus,) make sure that you accentuate the horn figures and build your solo around these figures. You don't have to nail each one, but do keep them firmly in your consciousness while you solo. You may notice that the time pushes a little bit during the drum solo section. This is because we were recording without a "click track" and so the time "breathes" a bit. This is something that happens even in the most professional situations that you encounter. There is an excitement and forward push that can happen while musicians are playing "live". This should not pose a problem for you when you are soloing over this part yourself. Simply be aware of it.

Background on the song and the arrangement: Todd Anderson came up with this beautiful version of Irving Berlin's classic when he was working with master Latin percussionist/bandleader Ray Baretto. The song was performed many times by Baretto's group, though strangely enough it was never recorded. I am proud to have Todd's masterpiece on my CD.

Summertime

Latin Jazz
"Cha cha"

[Track 2]

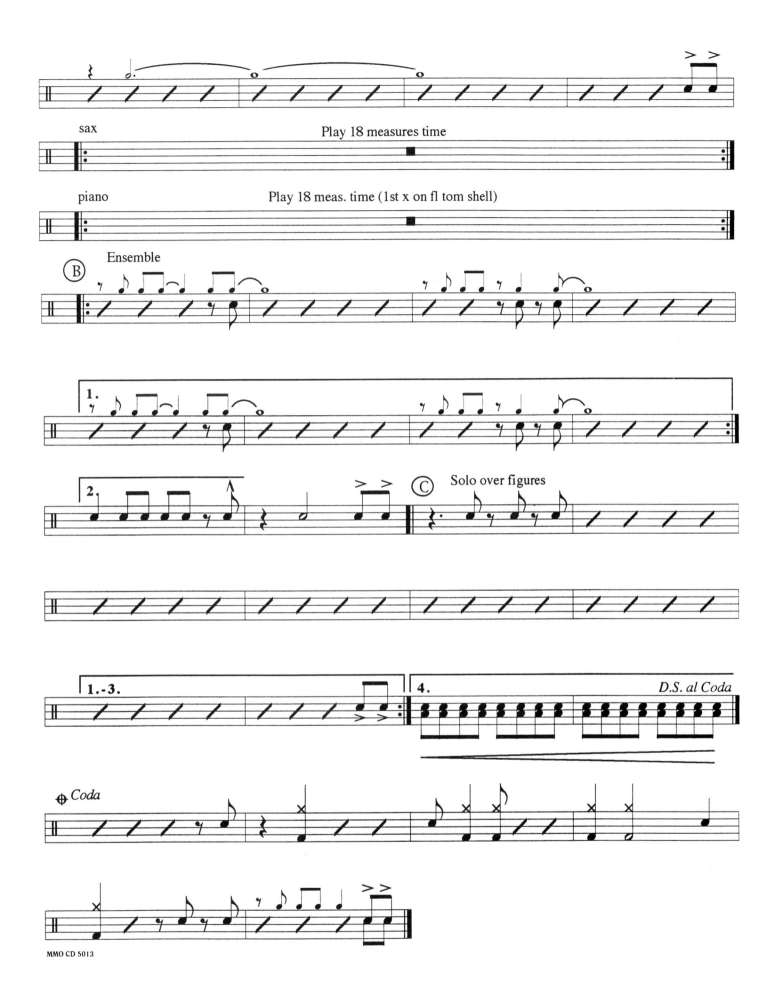

sax

Play 18 measures time

piano

Play 18 meas. time (1st x on fl tom shell)

B Ensemble

1.

2. C Solo over figures

1.-3. 4. D.S. al Coda

Coda

Concepts and performance tips: This is possibly the most challenging tune of this selection in terms of unexpected rhythmic phrasing and unusual solo form. Also, the accent scheme Kevin created is tricky at first. The concept of supporting the solos (which in this case is piano, followed by drums over the repeated 'A' section toward the end) is to suggest the accents of the melody and imply the rhythm section "hits" underneath the soloist. To put it another way, when first learning this tune you must stick pretty closely to the written music until you feel that you've internalized the accents and hits.

Once you get familiar with 'Chickory Stick', it begins to feel quite natural. The tune does indeed swing when played with the right feel. Just be wary of the 3/4 time bars, which occur in the 5th and 6th bars of the first 'A' section and in the 3rd and 4th bars of the last 'A'. These meter changes become second nature as you play through the tune several times.

After the first head, which follows an ABBA form, there is a piano solo over the entire form for which lasts a total of 3 choruses.

Then, the horns come in for the melody on the 'A' section as in the beginning, but when the last 'B' section comes around it is repeated as a rhythmic underpinning for a drum solo. This 8-bar section is repeated a total of 7 times; the first 5 times the accompaniment is piano and bass only. The horns join in for two more 8-bar cycles before ending the tune with the last 'A'. During this solo section it seemed as though musically this would be a great spot to play around with some over-the-barline phrasing and some odd-meters superimposed over the groove, since the rhythm was so solid with Sean and Kevin laying down this repeating 8-bar figure.

When the horns came back in, it felt like a good place to begin winding the solo down and so I was mainly slamming the groove at that point (with a few demented fills thrown in for good measure!). However, it could also be a place in which you build even more and solo even more strongly over the horns. Experiment here with trying different shapes to your solo, bringing it to a peak in slightly different spots each time you try it (as opposed to winding down in the same spot each time.)

Among the things explored in my solo were, in addition to odd-meter and over-the-barline things as mentioned previously, having some fun with choking the cymbal in my left hand. That way, my right hand remained free to try little melodic patterns around the set. I also took the opportunity to play around with some melodic triplet figures around the kit, at one point playing a figure (I thought later on) reminiscent of a Southern Italian Tarantella rhythm. The point I'm making here is that over a vamp like this you can really stretch out. Don't be worried about losing the groove or messing up; this is a play-along CD and not a live gig, and so it is the perfect time to "go out on a limb" musically and try things to see if they work!

Background on the song and the arrangement: Kevin Hays' composition can be also heard on his 1997 Blue Note records release, 'Andalucia'. It is a powerful and engaging rendition. The support and energy provided by the other two players in the trio, Jack DeJohnette on drums and the great Ron Carter on bass, is undeniable. I decided not to try and imitate Jack's approach to the song (since that is an impossible feat) but to have fun with it and be as creative as I could. The title, by the way, is a play on words of Chick Corea's name, as a tribute to him (as some of you may have guessed already!)

Chickory Stick

Medium/Uptempo Swing   [Track 3]

Piano solo for 3 choruses over form
then D.S. al Coda

Drum solo over figures (horns enter on 6th repeat)

rit.

Concepts and performance tips: In this era, the drummer is no longer confined to playing "swish swish" with the brushes on the snare drum for the duration of a piece when playing a jazz ballad. I first became aware of this when I attended a small-group workshop led by the great arranger Bill Finegan (who happens to be the father of our trumpet player.) The workshop was co-lead by guitarist Jim Hall. The philosophy taught by these masters regarding the drummer's approach to playing a ballad was that one can play a freer approach to the style, playing the drums and cymbals in a more open way without necessarily "stirring the soup"[1] the whole time.

I actually did use a swishing approach tofor part of this tune, but incorporated high hat splashes with the left foot and light, open cymbal work, as well as the occasional roll on a crash cymbal with my soft mallets. But for the concluding melody I switched to sticks and embellished the melody on the cymbals.

Perhaps the greatest examples demonstrating the use of sticks in a ballad can be heard on recordings featuring Jack DeJohnette on drums. He utilizes rapid single and double stroke rolls on the cymbals and plays in quite a "busy" (very active) way without ever "stepping on the toes" of the soloist or the melody.

Incidentally, the unison sixteenth notes that happen twice between the bass and drums on the full band version of the tune (during the last head) were completely spontaneous between us - we hadn't had any discussion in advance of what exactly we were going to play. The "open" approach to playing a ballad leaves room for all kinds of wonderful musical surprises!

The point is that you can try a variety of approaches when you play along with this tune. Try the whole piece with sticks, for example; or, play the head with soft mallets and play the remainder with brushes. You can even play the entire thing with a soft sweeping approach with brushes only, in the traditional style. When it comes to playing a ballad, the only requirements are that you play with sensetivity, play dynamically, and (most of the time) delicately. However, in professional situations, if a bandleader or arranger requests that you play the swishing sound on the snare with 2 & 4 on the high hat, it is usually good judgement to play what is asked of you. It's better to save your experimentation for situations in which you have the total freedom to play more openly.

Background on the song and the arrangement: Short Ballad is a composition by our bassist Sean Smith, and like many of his songs the melody is of key importance in the tune. This should be kept in mind when approaching this piece on the drums. Play to serve the melody, always listen to what's around you, and "handle with care"...

Short Ballad

Concepts and performance tips: Brazilian music has had a huge influence on the American music scene for over three decades. The combination of African influence, coupled with European harmony and melodic sensibility, is different than the way it was melted together here in the United States. The pulse and groove of music from Brazil is in some ways deeper and more organic, more earthy, than what we have come up with in North America. American music has more of a marching band influence, since jazz was originally played by brass bands in New Orleans nearly 100 years ago. In dance music and popular music coming out of Brazil, on the other hand, the African roots are only barely disguised.

With that in mind, I emphasize the steady 16th note flow on the high hat and ride, with variations according to what is going on around me (see chart for bass drum beat, or refer to the full-band CD.) I gave myself a fair amount of flexibility on the snare drum sidestick pattern in order to flow with what the other players were doing, while never losing sight of the basic pulse. The percussion tracks play more of a constant role, especially the shaker, which is an important component of Samba percussion groups in Rio De Janeiro. It is important to learn the basic samba bass drum pulse, which provides the heartbeat of the whole rhythmic picture along with the bass. In this "acoustic" concept, I played the bass drum lightly, but the feel of it is present in the music.

In fact, if you don't have much experience with Brazilian music, it is best to stick to the written beat provided in the drum chart and get comfortable with it. Once you really feel locked in with this, begin to experiment and play around with different accents and rhythmic variations within the groove. Please note in the full band version that although I take quite a few liberties in terms of fill-ins and accenting, every note that I play is relevant to the basic underlying groove of the song and the style.

Also remember to bring your volume level down at the beginning of the sax solo, which follows the piano solo (refer to the Instructional Notes for the song "Night".) One of the focal points of playing samba is to keep the drive and forward motion of the music alive while at the same time varying the dynamic levels. Remember, the drummer has the greatest ability of all band members to vary dynamic levels, from extremely soft to very loud. Use this position with care and sensitivity! Nothing turns me off more, as a listener, than to go to a jazz club, eager to experience a group of musicians who are connecting and flowing together, only to find the balance thrown off by a drummer who bashes mercilessly at the first opportunity without caring to explore the softer end of the spectrum. Even the greatest drummers on earth fall prey to this habit at times!

So have fun with varying dynamics when playing along with Blue Bossa. Another area to do this is in the intro, a repeating 4-bar phrase which is to be played forte [loud] the first time and piano [soft] when it repeats. This 8-bar section repeats again after the head, and once again at the very end of the tune.

The solo section gives you an to play some creative fills, while accenting ensemble figures opportunity (similar to the drum solo section in 'Summertime'). This section consists of a 16-bar phrase (one chorus) repeating twice. The difference between your approach to this solo part and the one in 'Summertime' is that this time you should try to play each horn figure in unison [together] with the ensemble for maximum effectiveness and excitement, whereas in 'Summertime' the ensemble figures in the drum solo section are more of a background pattern to play off of in your solo.

Background on the song and the arrangement: Todd Anderson's arrangement of Blue Bossa, the frequently-played standard written by Kenny Dorham, was part of the early wave of Brazilian influence on the American Jazz scene. Another notable example is 'Girl From Ipanema' as recorded by Antonio Carlos Jobim and Stan Getz during the same era as Joe's classic, the early 1960's. If you are interested in pursuing this genre further, I suggest that you seek out 'Elis Regina Live in Montreaux', a recording by the late and great vocalist, which features the brilliant Paulo Braga on drums. Also, Duduka Da Fonseca, Portinho, and Airto Moreira are other master Brazilian drummers to pay attention to (Airto is primarily known as a percussionist but is a fiery drumset player as well.)

Blue Bossa

Samba/Bossa Nova   [Track 5]

14

Piano   Play 32 Bars Time*

(Horns)

etc.   (8)

(12)

(16)

Sax solo   Play 32 Bars Time   Play 31 Bars Time   Fill

*<u>Note</u>: You can switch from hi hat to ride cymbal during solos

MMO CD 5013

Solo

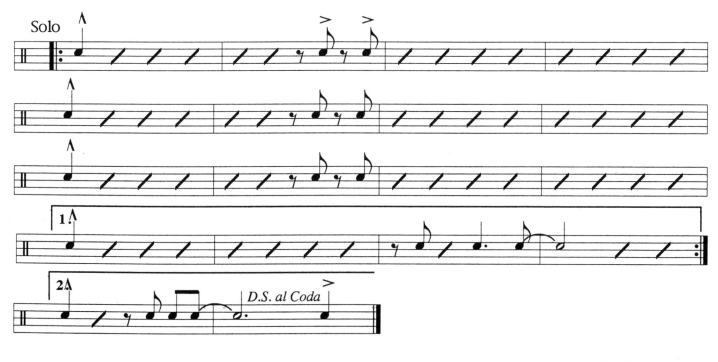

D.S. al Coda

Coda

mp

MMO CD 5013

Concepts and performance tips: One of the elements to focus on here is the art of accompanying a bass solo on drums. I decided in this case to accompany Sean Smith's exquisite two-chorus solo with sticks, choosing delicate cymbal work to embellish his melodic and very compositional approach to soloing. You are certainly under no obligation to take this route though it may be fun to try if that is not familiar territory for you. You may of course also try brushes on cymbals only, brushes on snare only...or you may choose to "lay out" [not play] altogether to allow the harmonic nuances of the bass to really leap out. Experiment and have fun with this - as mentioned elsewhere in this book, the drummer is no longer required to play only "swish swish" with the brushes here. Just remember to always listen and be extra aware of what's happening around you musically, and how the drums fit into the picture.

Following the tenor sax and bass solos, there is a drum break in which you can solo around some ensemble figures, similar to what you might encounter in a big band chart. I usually follow a "mini big band" concept when I see something like this in a chart. That means I try to "set up" the rhythmic figures with short fills, to "announce" upcoming phrases and give some shape to the overall phrasing of the ensemble lines. [Also, horn players and the other musicians find it helpful to feel the rhythm of a phrase when the drummer does this.] In other words, I see it as both a drum feature and an ensemble feature in one. This keeps my soloing pertinent to what is going on around me. This view also enables me to enhance the overall group sound while at the same time having some creative fun. In this particular solo section, I found it effective to leave a few silent beats to allow a "breath" before the return of the melody.

Background on the song and the arrangement: Todd Anderson came up with this clever arrangement on Joe Henderson's classic and ageless standard. This tune still gets called a lot at jam sessions. Check out the exciting big band version of it on the 1996 Verve release "Joe Henderson Big Band".

Serenity

MMO CD 5013

Style: "Straight eighth feel"/Jazz Bossa Nova [sometimes referred to as an "ECM" feel, in reference to the rhythmic concept frequently featured on recordings from the German record label ECM during the 1970's-80's].

Concepts and performance tips: This sing-song kind of tune presented by our bassist Sean Smith is in a now-standard "straight eighth" rhythmic mode, reminiscent of a Bossa Nova beat [the classic Brazilian style pioneered by such great composer/instrumentalists as Antonio Carlos Jobim and Baden Powell in the 1960's]. The underlying drum groove is characterized by straight (as opposed to "swung") eighth notes on the ride cymbal or high-hat and straight quarter notes on the snare drum, played as a "sidestick" or "rim click" beat [2].

I decided that it would be a nice change of scenery to put the bass solo first in the line-up, since It is such a matter of habit to have the horns solo first, followed by bass, and drums getting a little in at the end, and so on. It is crucial to try and break the typical and come up with nice alternatives to habitual formats when you get together with friends to play, or with your band. Jazz is one of the great symbols of American originality, so why fall into stale old ways? Of course, the drums do solo last in this particular case, but it fits the musical scheme to do so in this case! [excuses, excuses....]

My approach to accompanying the bass solo here was to play colors on the cymbals and the rest of the kit with brushes (as opposed to sticks - see notes for "Short Ballad").

NOTE: One of the key elements of being a complete jazz drummer is to train yourself to switch seamlessly from sticks to brushes and back. A true wizard at this was "Philly" Joe Jones, as well as Art Blakey. It seemed as though they could snatch a stick or a brush from mid-air, while in fact

it was a practiced art and each player develops her or his own approach. I personally use a technique I borrowed from the great Alan Dawson, which is to keep the brushes concealed under your left or right thigh (that's right, you actually sit on them) if you know you will need them, and use one hand to pull them out while continuing to keep time with the other. Then, you take the space of about one quarter note to make the switch and end up right into the groove without interruption. The drum solo feature in this tune is played over the main "hook"[3] of the tune, which is the repeating 4-bar rhythmic motif stated at the very top of the tune. The whole cycle is eight bars in length, and repeats four times altogether, which means that you have thirty-two bars altogether to make your solo statement (over a full-ensemble "vamp"[4]). Notice that after the 32 bars is complete, I cue the band that my solo has come to a close by playing 4 bars of straight time, followed by 4 bars of playing the vamp pretty much in unison with the band to bring the tune to its conclusion. Also, notice that there is a slight ritard (slowing down) for the final two bars of the piece. This will feel natural and you will stay together with the group in this ending simply by listening carefully as you play - the number one "rule" of playing this music!

Background on the song and the arrangement: Sean Smith wrote this song several years ago and it has been recorded numerous times by different artists, but the definitive version can be heard on the 1996 Koch label release "A Good Thing", by alto saxophonist Alan Mezquida. If you do check out this CD, which I highly recommend, pay special attention to the wonderful work of rising drum and percussion star Leon Parker. Leon is a very creative player and is a master of subtlety and restraint, and makes a lot of music on his now-famous super minimal drum kit.

Revelation

Straight 8th Feel   [Track 7]

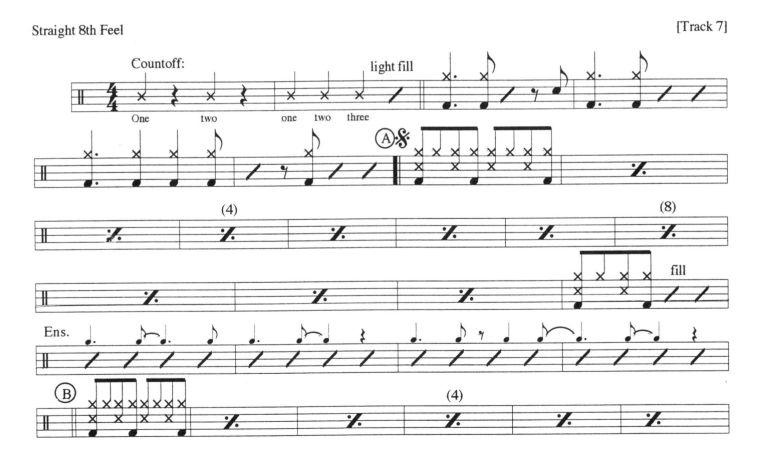

19

POOLSIDE BLUES [TRACK 8]

Concepts and performance tips: Nobody could shuffle like the late Art Blakey and this is my tribute to him. He was also the possessor of the meanest press roll5 on the planet, and created a way of incorporating the two in an unforgettable way. I snuck one in after the second of four choruses in Jamie Finegan's trumpet solo. Another master of the shuffle is Steve Gadd.

The idea of playing an effective Jazz shuffle is to play a two-and-four backbeat on the snare with a ghost note preceding each snare hit. This way, you get the effect of an unbroken eighth notes (with, of course, a swing feel, not straight eighths.) The feel should have a forward-motion feel to it [though not necessarily played "on top" of the beat], and and should be kept as simple as possible.

It is also effective to play eighth-note triplet fills. This is a great device for leading out of a solo, connecting phrases, or introducing a new soloist. Count Basie's drummer during the 1950's-60's, Sonny Payne, was one of the true masters of utilizing big, crescendo'd triplet fills in just the right spots.

Make sure to "set up" the interlude which follows the melody and also happens between the two horn solos (it is a repeat of the intro phrase,) which gives you a perfect opportunity to try one of these triplet fills since there is a 4-bar space to take a fill. At the end of this four bar spot (the last two beats,) leave an empty space in your fill to accommodate the melody (as per the chart.) It is crucial to let the horns have this opening moment of the intro figure alone; it is sometimes as important to know when not to play as when you should be playing.

But the real key to making this tune happen is plain and direct: you must groove your socks off! Put all of yourself into the beat, and be creative in figuring out when to give extra forward motion to the groove (play "ahead of the beat") and when to relax it and lay back (playing "behind the beat".) When you bring the right spirit into playing a shuffle, you can really inspire the other musicians to new heights.

Background on the song and the arrangement: This is an original tune by Todd Anderson. The arrangement is reminiscent of the classic Art Blakey And The Jazz Messengers shuffles in the 50's and 60's (such as 'Blues March') though Art continued his indomitable groove well past the classic "hard bop" era of the 50's.

Poolside Blues

Blakey Shuffle

[Track 8]

MMO CD 5013

21

Concept: This tune was designed to give drummers a chance to stretch out over a standard 12-bar blues bass line. Following the opening melody of two choruses in length (a total of 24 bars), the idea is to "trade" choruses (of 12 bars in length) with another drummer (in this case me). [NOTE: a "chorus" is the grouping of bars which consitutes the repeating cycle of a tune.]

After trading three whole choruses, starting with mine and followed by you, the solo length cut down to "trading fours", exchanging solo breaks of four bars in length, for two choruses. Then, you will trade two-bar breaks for two more choruses, one-bar breaks for two choruses, and the melody is repeated for the finish, topped off with a classic Duke Ellington-style ending.

I realize that this all sounds very complicated, but it really isn't. It breaks down like this:

- "Head" (melody) twice;
- Trade choruses three times;
- Trade fours (four-bar breaks) for two choruses;
- Trade two's (two-bar breaks) for two choruses;
- Trade one bar breaks for two choruses;
- Head out twice

It may take a few tries, but the idea is to have fun and not worry about necessarily nailing it the first time.

Performance tips: Try to learn the drum melody and play it along with me (see the drum charts included in this package). Also, it can be played simply with trading and not playing the melody; this might be easier at first.

Additionally, it is fun to try playing exactly some of the figures I did, as a type of "ear training" and a challenge to yourself. In other words, when I play a four-bar break, you use the following four bars of solo space (YOUR turn to solo) to copy "note-for-note" what I just played in the recording. [NOTE: It's great to try this kind of thing with other drummers; it's good practice to get two drum kits together and experiment with two players. Some of my most exhilarating moments in my early days were jamming with a second drummer.]

Background on the song and the arrangement: It was modeled after the concept made famous on the classic Buddy Rich/Gene Krupa recording on the Verve label, "The Drum Battle" (now available on CD.) The big difference is that I borrowed from the innovative master Max Roach and played with Sean Smith's bass line, which is more "musical" than to use a click or some other sound to provide the time during the solo spots.

Also, soloing over a bass line assists the drummer in continually keeping the song and the form in mind. It helps the drum soloist to make a musical statement which is more pertinent to the whole picture of the tune, as opposed to merely bashing out a solo and then counting out loud for the other musicians to come back in together. Therefore, this tune is good basic practice for drummers in the art of staying with the song form while soloing.

Now we're ready to go for it! Review the full band CD, then pop on your 'phones and give it a run for yourself. Or, go right ahead to the minus drums CD and play your heart out with these great musicians. There is no prescribed approach. Use the +drums CD and the information on these pages a reference and a guide, or review everything carefully before you dive in. Either way, I hope that you have some fun with it and learn something while your at it.

Each time you practice, you should be a better musician than you were before you started the session, if you are using your practice time wisely. It's not the sheer number of hours you put in which make you a better musician; it's the SUBSTANCE of your practice time, the content. Good luck!

Count Me In

Uptempo Swing (Drum/Bass duet)

count: (stick clicks)

solo (1 chorus)

repeat 2 x's

"4's"   4   solo   repeat 2 x's

"2's"   2   solo   2   solo   repeat 2 x's

"1's"

D.S. al Coda   Coda

MMO CD 5013

*Optional- play <u>time</u> under other soloist

MUSIC MINUS ONE DRUMMER

Night · Summertime · Chickory Stick
Short Ballad · Blue Bossa
Serenity · Revelation
Poolside Blues · Count Me In

5013

OPEN SESSION

with the
Greg Burrows Quintet

EVANS
RESONANT

MMO Music Group • 50 Executive Boulevard, Elmsford, New York 10523, 1-(800) 669-7464
Website: www. minusone.com • E-mail: mmomus@aol.com